SOME KIND OF LOVE STORY

by
Arthur Miller

**DRAMATISTS
PLAY SERVICE
INC.**

SOME KIND OF LOVE STORY, in tandem with ELEGY FOR A LADY, was presented by the Long Wharf Theater in New Haven, Connecticut, in November, 1982 under the omnibus title of 2 BY A.M. The production was directed by the author, with Christine Lahti and Charles Cioffi appearing in both plays. The sets were by Hugh Landwehr; costumes were by Bill Walker; and the lighting was by Ronald Wallace.

Note: ELEGY FOR A LADY is published by Dramatists Play Service in a separate edition.

AUTHOR'S NOTE

The stories and characters of this pair of plays are unrelated to one another but in different ways both works are passionate voyages through the masks of illusion to an ultimate reality. In *Some Kind of Love Story* it is social reality and the corruption of justice which a delusionary woman both conceals and unveils. The search in *Elegy for a Lady* is for the shape and meaning of a sexual relationship that is being brought to a close by a lover's probable death. In both the unreal is an agony to be striven against and, at the same time, accepted as life's condition.

3

CAST

ANGELA
TOM O'TOOLE

The action takes place in Angela's bedroom, in an American city.

TIME: The present.

SOME KIND OF LOVE STORY

ACT I

*A bed in a darkened room. A window. The head-
board of the bed is white plastic tufting with gold
trim, Grand Rapids Baroque. A door Upstage to the
bathroom. Another at Right to Living Room. Skirts,
bras, shoes, articles of clothing dropped everywhere.
Angela is barely visible sitting up on the bed. The
Right door opens.*

Tom O'Toole sticks his head in.

TOM. Are we decent?

ANGELA. Christ's sake, close the door.

TOM. Lemme get in first! (*Shuts door behind him. Pushes
back his narrow brimmed hat, unbuttons his raincoat, and is
forced to peer through the murky air to see her face.*)
Well! — You're sounding nice and spunky, how's it goin'
tonight?

ANGELA. Philly out there?

TOM. In the kitchenette, lip-readin' his racin' form.

ANGELA. Say anything to you?

TOM. Nooo. Just laid one of his outraged-husband looks on
me again. What do you say I buy you a spaghetti? — Come
on.

ANGELA. You can turn on the light. And lock the door, will you?

TOM. What's with the rollers? You going out? (*She undoes a roller now that her attention has been drawn to it. He locks the door and switches a lamp on. She is sitting up in bed, permed hair, black slip, pink wrapper. Lights a cigarette. Tom, continuing.*) Jeeze, you really are swollen. You want ice?

ANGELA. (*Works her jaw, touching it.*) It's going down.

TOM. (*Sitting on a stool beside bed.*) Hope you don't mind, darlin', but a man who takes his fists to his wife ought to be strung up by his testicles one at a time.

ANGELA. (*A preoccupied air.*) Nobody's perfect. He can't help himself, he's immature.

TOM. Well, maybe I'll understand it sometime — It's amazing, I always leave here with more questions than I came in with.

ANGELA. He's still the father of my daughter. (*Gets off bed, tidies up the room a bit.*) By the way, she called me from L.A. She's going to apply to the University of California, being she's so fantastic in basketball.

TOM. (*Dropping into a chair, hat and coat still on.*) Well, that'd be nice, wouldn't it. You're lucky to have a kid these days who loves you.

ANGELA. Don't yours?

TOM. Yeah, but they're exceptional. Anyway, I'm unusually loveable. (*He guffaws.*)

ANGELA. What're you laughing at? — It's true. (*Sadly.*) You're probably the most loveable man I've ever met.

TOM. (*To get down to business.*) You caught me climbin' into bed when you called.

ANGELA. I appreciate you coming, Tom — this had to be my worst day yet. (*She moves to window to look into the backyard.*)

TOM. No kiddin'. On the phone you sounded like you seen a ghost.

ANGELA. (*A wan smile.*) You ever going to love me again?

TOM. Always will, honey—in spirit. (*The answer turns her sadder; she restlessly walks in sighing frustration.*) I explained it, Ange—

ANGELA. What'd you explain?

TOM. You are part of the case in a certain way; and I can't be concentrating on this case and banging you at the same time. It's all wrong. I'm being as straight as I can with you.—What happened today?

ANGELA. I don't know—it just hit me again like a ton of bricks that Felix is still sitting in that cell.

TOM. That's right; it'll be five years October.

ANGELA. You tend to get used to it after so long but today I simply . . . I couldn't stand it all over again.

TOM. I can't stand it *every* day.

ANGELA. (*As though re-awakened to his value.*) You're a wonderful man, Tom. You're really one of a kind.

TOM. Personally, I wouldn't mind sharin' the distinction, but I don't see too many volunteers on *this* case.

ANGELA. (*She looks off, shaking her head with wonder at his character.*) Be proud of yourself—I mean with all the great people in this state, the colleges, the churches, the newspapers, and nobody lifts a finger except you . . . I simply can't believe he's still in there!

TOM. (*Sensing attenuation.*) What'd you want to see me about, Ange?

ANGELA. (*Glances at him, then gets up again, moves.*) I'm really teetering. My skin is so tight I could scream.

TOM. What happened today?

ANGELA. God how I love to see you sitting here and the sound of your voice . . . (*At the window.*) . . . Is that drizzle comin' down again?

TOM. But it's kind of warm out; you want to try to walk it off? Come on, I'll take you to the boardwalk, buy you a chowder.

ANGELA. (*Moves restlessly.*) God, how I hate this climate.

TOM. I thought it reminded you of Sweden.

ANGELA. I'm a Finn, not a Swede; I said it was *like* Finland—Not that I was ever *in* Finland.

TOM. (*A grin.*) So how's my standing tonight?

ANGELA. You're always in my top three; you know that.

TOM. (*Wryly.*) Not always, Ange—last time I was practically wiped off the scoreboard.

ANGELA. (*Genuinely surprised.*) What are you talking about?

TOM. You ordered me never to show my face again, don't you remember?

ANGELA. (*Vaguely recalling a probability.*) Well, you were probably pressuring me, that's all; I will not submit to pressure . . .

TOM. Well, *you* called *me* tonight, kid. So what's it about?

ANGELA. What the hell is this goddam rush, suddenly?

TOM. (*Laughs.*) Rush! You have any idea how long we've been bullshitting around together about this case? It's damn near five years!

ANGELA. And every single thing you know about it came from me and don't you forget it either.

TOM. Well . . . not everything . . .

ANGELA. (*A shot of angry indignation.*) *Everything*!

TOM. (*A sigh.*) Well, all right.—But I'm still nowhere.

ANGELA. This is a whole new side of you, isn't it?

TOM. (*Sensing her fear—gently.*) Baby Doll, the last time on Thursday I spent seven-and-one-half hours in this room with you . . .

ANGELA. It was nowhere *near* seven and . . .

TOM. (*Suppressing explosion.*) Until two-thirty A.M. when you give me such a kick in the balls that if it'd landed I'd have gone into orbit. So we can call tonight a strictly professional visit to hear whatever you got to say about the case of Felix Epstein . . . and *nothing else.*—Now what'd you want to tell me?

ANGELA. (*Dismissing him.*) Well, I can't talk to you in a

8

mechanical atmosphere.

TOM. (*Gets up.*) Then goodnight and happy dreams.

ANGELA. What are you doing?

TOM. (*A strained laugh.*) Gettin' back into my pajamas! —I have driven here through half an hour of fog and rain!

ANGELA. (*Open helplessness.*) I'm desperate to talk to you! Why don't you give me a chance to open my mouth? (*Turning her back on him, moving . . .*) I mean, shit, if you want a mechanical conversation go see your friendly Ford dealer.

TOM. I'll tell you something, Angela—you're just lucky I'm still in love with you.

ANGELA. (*She smiles now, tragically.*) You wouldn't be kidding about that if I wasn't a sick woman—I'd have walked you off into the sunset five years ago and don't think I couldn't have done it.

TOM. My wife thinks you could still do it.

ANGELA. Go on, she knows why you see me nowadays.

TOM. Maybe that's why she's talkin' separation.

ANGELA. One of the nicest things about you, Tom, is that you're so obvious when you're full of shit.

TOM. She thinks we're still making it, Angela.

ANGELA. (*Breaks into a smile, warm and pleasured, gets up and comes to him, takes off his hat and kisses the top of his head.*) Honestly?

TOM. I mean it. From the way I talk about you she says she can tell.

ANGELA. (*Sliding her hand toward his crotch.*) Well as long as she believes it, why don't we, again?

TOM. (*Grasping her wrists.*) Y'know . . . I had to give up the booze twenty years ago, and then the cigarettes because the doctor told me I have the makeup of an addict. If I went into you again I'd never come out the rest of my life.

ANGELA. (*Seizing the respite.*) Were you ever really in love, Tom?

TOM. (*Hesitates, then nods.*) Once.

ANGELA. I don't mean as a kid . . .

TOM. No, I was about twenty-five.

ANGELA. What happened to her?

TOM. (*Hesitates, then grins in embarrassment.*) My mother didn't approve.

ANGELA. Why not, she wasn't Catholic?

TOM. She was Catholic.

ANGELA. (*A wide grin.*) A tramp?

TOM. No! But she knew I'd stayed over with her a couple of times. And we were a strict family, see.

ANGELA. You've still got a lot of priest in you, Tom — I love that about you.

TOM. You do? I don't. Leaving that woman was the biggest mistake I ever made. In fact, five or six years later, I was already married but I went back looking for her — I was ready to leave my wife — But she was gone, nobody knew where.

ANGELA. (*Romantically.*) And you really still think of her?

TOM. More now than ever. In that respect I lived the wrong life.

ANGELA. (*She is staring at him, an open expression on her face. On her knees beside his chair she rests her head on his shoulder.*) Life is so wrong — a man like you ought to be happy all day and all night long. (*Angela sings "When Irish Eyes Are Smiling". He corrects a couple of mistakes.*)

TOM. (*Intimately, breaking into the song.*) Tell me the truth, Angela — are you ever going to unload what you know about the Epstein case?

ANGELA. (*Slight pause. She is deeply fearful, but taking pleasure, too, in his concern.*) I'm so worried about myself, Tom. I think I did some kind of a number today, right in the middle of Crowley Square.

TOM. (*Grinning.*) I know when you're changing the subject, kid.

ANGELA. (*Angered.*) It scared me to death, for Christ's sake! — I'm still shaking!

TOM. What happened?

ANGELA. (*A moment to let her indignation sink in.*) I'm

10

walking along past the piano store — Ramsey's?

TOM. And?

ANGELA. All I remember next is I'm sitting on the fender of a parked car with a whole crowd of people around me. A couple of young guys were sniggering — like I'd done something indecent or something — they had that look, y'know? (*A deepening of overtly fearful breathing.*) I've really got to get to a doctor, Tom.

TOM. Okay.

ANGELA. I go blotto for longer and longer stretches, I think. Sometimes I get the feeling that I don't know where the hell I been all day, or what I said, or to who I said it.

TOM. You want me to arrange a psychiatrist?

ANGELA. With what, though?

TOM. Maybe I can get one on the tab. You want one?

ANGELA. (*A sigh.*) I don't know, everyone I ever went to ends up trying to get into my pants. Anyway, I know what they'll tell me — I'm a schizophrenic. So what else is new? Why are you so resentful tonight?

TOM. Honey, it's the same schizophrenia conversation we had fifteen different times, and it's eleven P.M.

ANGELA. What I am trying to tell you is that my heart is hanging by a thread, I haven't got very long. Or is that important?

TOM. Then why don't you tell me what you know before it's too late? The man is still innocent and he's still dying by inches in prison; his wife is a walking wreck, his parents are ready for the morgue, and you have the key to this case, Angela — I know it as sure as I know my name — and you jerk me around month after month, a crumb here a crumb there. . . . I'm so exhausted I can't sleep! — And now you take to dragging me out of bed every other night to chat me up? (*She covers her eyes suddenly.*) Maybe it'd be good if you saw Felix again — you haven't been up there in a year, I could drive you . . .

ANGELA. (*This touched a nerve.*) I don't want to see him.

11

TOM. (*Surprised.*) You mean *never?*

ANGELA. I've done more for Felix Epstein than you or anybody. I led the fight all by myself, for Christ's sake!

TOM. Honey, I don't know too much about the head, but as one ex-Catholic to another . . .

ANGELA. I'm not "ex."

TOM. Well, semi-ex. What's eatin' you alive is not schizophrenia, kid, it's your conscience.

ANGELA. (*With shaky sarcasm.*) You been talking to your friendly Jewish psychiatrist again, I see.

TOM. He's not my psychiatrist, he's interested in the case.

ANGELA. Well if that's what he thinks I'm up to, you can tell him from me he's full of shit.

TOM. I'll send him an immediate wire. (*Makes to leave.*) I'm really beat . . .

ANGELA. (*Instantly stopping him.*) Wait, I just want you to tell me one thing. Sit down a second. Don't be this way — (*They sit.*) Why are you on this case.

TOM. (*Shocked — a near screech.*) *What*!!

ANGELA. (*Sharply.*) Well, don't be mad, I'm trying to tune myself! They're yelling tonight.

TOM. (*Quieting.*) You're hearing them now? (*She nods. He is awkward making this absurdly obvious explanation.*) Well, the Epsteins hired me to clear Felix, they paid me five thousand dollars. — How do you pop a question like that after all these years?

ANGELA. Simply that if I told you what I know . . . (*A near stutter.*) . . . what, what . . . when would I ever see you again — on television? The great detective who broke the Epstein case . . . ?

TOM. In other words you backed me out of my pajamas to be the Ladies Home Companion again. (*He starts angrily for the door, but she flies to him in what he sees is a genuine terror.*)

ANGELA. No! Tom, you can't go! Oh, God you can't leave me tonight . . . Tom, Tom, please, you mustn't . . . ! Not

12

tonight! (*She has a grip on him and pulls him back to the chair, forcing him into it.*) . . . you got to stay . . . just a little while . . .

TOM. God Almighty, what has got you so scared? (*Trembling, she returns to sit on the bed.*)

ANGELA. Let's just be peaceful a while, okay? (*Making conversation.*) What . . . what's it like out?

TOM. (*Reaching into his side pocket, ignoring her question.*) You know what I done?

ANGELA. (*Grateful for the diversion, smiles, mimicking.*) What'd you done?

TOM. Finally bought myself a notebook . . . (*Takes out a black looseleaf notebook.*) This is amazing—you askin' me why I'm in the case—because I sat down after lunch and started making a resume of the case right from day-one, and it suddenly jumped off the page at me. (*A grin.*) That I had no explanation why *you* were involved in this case in the first place. At all and whatsoever. That funny?

ANGELA. Why shouldn't I be?

TOM. But why should you be, honey? (*A grinding laugh.*) You never knew Felix before his arrest; *or* the parents. And there you were in the courtroom every single day of the trial, and startin' up a defense committee yet!—I'd just always taken it for granted that you belonged there!

ANGELA. Why not?—I had nothing to do in the daytime and I kept reading about the case in the papers so I came to see. (*He glances up at her with a look of open skepticism.*) Why don't you come out with it? (*She is almost visibly swept by a furiously pleasurable release, a sense of her real self; she stands, throwing out one hip, arms akimbo, mouth distorted into a tough sneer and her voice goes rough as gravel.*) What you mean is how does a fuckin' whore come off attending a . . .

TOM. Now wait, I did not call you a . . .

ANGELA. Go on, you're full of shit—you know I've been a hooker!

TOM. I never said . . .

ANGELA. Oh, fuck off, will ya! You've snooped around, say it! — I've hooked the Holiday Inn, Travelodge . . .

TOM. Cut it out, Angela . . .

ANGELA. . . . Howard Johnson's, Ramada Inn . . . I've spread my ass on every barstool in this misbegotten, reamed-out village . . . why don't you say it?

TOM. (*Helplessly.*) I did not mean that you . . .

ANGELA. Say it! — How does a common slut *presume* . . . .

TOM. (*Erupting.*) I did not cast any such aspersion, Angela . . . !

ANGELA. (*Bending over to shout.*) . . . *Presume* to involve herself in high class causes!

TOM. (*Mystified and alarmed.*) What *is* this?

ANGELA. (*She seems actually blind, enraged.*) Well, you can get your filthy parish mind off my ass, you Irish mutt!

TOM. (*Suddenly aware, stepping back from her.*) . . . Oh, God, is this a number?

ANGELA. (*Cupping her breasts to thrust them forward, mimics him.*) "Oh, God!" Grab onto this you jerked-off choir boy . . . come on, get your finger out of your yum-yum and try some of this!

TOM. (*Holding his head.*) Holy God.

ANGELA. Go on, you don't kid me . . . (*Turning and trying to force his hand onto her buttocks.*) Grab hold, you fucking milk-face, you think you're better than anybody else?

TOM. Angela, Jesus . . . ! (*A struggle; he forces her onto the bed. She screams and tries to fight him off, loses her wind, and gasping, as he stands up, watching him . . . pushing his hand off.*)

ANGELA. Well, if you can't get it up get goin'. I've got a line into the street tonight. Tip the hatcheck girl — if you can part with a dollar. And the name is Leontine in case you want to ask for me next time. (*She has gradually lost an inner pressure and seems to fall asleep. O'Toole goes and bends over her, moved and mystified. Draws a blanket over her.*

14

Then he straightens up and peers into the air, goes to the phone and dials.)

TOM. (*Sotto voce, with glances toward the bed.*) Hello? That you Mrs. Levy? Tom O'Toole here. (*Charmingly.*) You sounded like your daughter! — Oh, pretty fair, thanks; the doctor said I could call anytime and I . . . — Oh, thanks very much, I'm really sorry for the hour. — Really! — I never thought you people watched TV! Thanks. (*Waits, glances over to Angela, then stares front with a certain eagerness.*) Hey, Josh, how are ya! — (*Nods.*) I'm there now but I might have to hang up, she just blew herself out. — Yeah, just like I described to you. Listen, I just got an idea. — Bad, very bad; really, really off the wall tonight, maybe the worst yet; in fact she just did a new one on me that I never saw before; Leontine, a real house whore. Horrendous vulgarity; you know, right off the knuckles. Listen, I gotta be quick — something just struck me; could a person have delusions, but like inside the delusion is the facts? What I'm trying to say, Josh . . . is that I got a gut feeling tonight that *somebody might really be threatening her life.* — Hell, I don't *know* why, but it's very hard to watch her and believe that she's stoking the whole thing up from inside, you see? I mean if they really want to get rid of her it verifies a lot of what she's been saying, you see? — Right! 'Cause I can't help it, Josh, I still believe that the key to this case is under that pantyhose. (*Listens avidly.*) Oh, she's definitely had Mob connections, that's objective; Johnny Gates kept her something like two years. — Gates? He's the head honcho. Numero Uno. But I checked the apartment house myself and she used to live there, no questions about it. — Listen, I might've given you the wrong idea — everything factual she's told me has stacked up with my own information. (*Laughs.*) No-no, I've got great respect for fantasy; look, I was six years on the New York Vice Squad, how fantastic can you get? — Yes, please, go ahead. (*Listens.*) In what sense, my relation? (*Blushingly.*) Well, you must've guessed, didn't you? We rolled around together last Spring

15

but I finally decided to go back to the *status quo ante.* —
Well, I got some bad feelings; started to wonder if they had
her back working for them again. —Ya, basically prostitu-
tion. In fact, I think hubby may be the pimp, he's been
punching her around again lately and that's typical pimp
relationship. —Ya, but I thought she'd gotten out of that a
long time ago. Even on the Vice Squad as a young guy I never
touched them; I don't even like public swimming pools!
(*Sees Angela moving.*) She's moving around . . . —I read you
. . . but see she's got some terrific perceptions, sees right
through you to your spinal cord . . . she can be terrific company, wonderful sense of humor . . . I mean she's not *always*
crazy. —But I think I'm *being* objective; maybe sometimes
you've got to go to crazy people for the facts, though . . .
maybe facts are what's making them crazy unless I'm bananas
too, by this time. (*She is sitting up, looking around.*) Gotta
go. (*He hangs up.*) How you doin', dear? (*She turns to him,
sharp surprise.*) . . . I been here a few minutes.
ANGELA. How long you been here?
TOM. Few minutes.
ANGELA. Was that Philly knocking?
TOM. I didn't hear any knocking, you must've been
dreaming.
ANGELA. (*Slight pause—she stares at door.*) Would you go
and see if they're still out there?
TOM. Who's that, dear?
ANGELA. The cops.
TOM. What cops you mean?
ANGELA. The cruiser. They've been parking a cruiser on the
street almost all the time. Didn't you see it when you came?
TOM. . . . Well, no, I didn't notice.
ANGELA. Well, go and take a look out front. Go ahead.
TOM. (*Suspending disbelief hoping it is true.*) Okay. (*He
unlocks door, exits, as . . .*)
ANGELA. Look out the bay window—usually toward Rod-

16

man Street. (*She turns front, fear in her face, an attempt at concentration . . . he re-enters, shuts door and walks into the room. She rather quickly goes and locks the door, always glancing at him for his report.*)

TOM. Don't see any cruiser, Angela.

ANGELA. Well, believe me, they're always there.

TOM. (*Nods . . . only half-pretending to disbelieve her.*) Cops are leaning on you? (*She barely nods, turns away.*) When did *this* start?

ANGELA. About . . . three, four weeks.

TOM. You mean since I began coming around so much again?

ANGELA. I think so.

TOM. Well, that would be nice, if I'm makin' them nervous. But I have to say it, honey—there's no cruiser down there now.

ANGELA. You're . . . not leaving, are you?

TOM. I'll stay a few minutes, if you want. (*Removes his coat. She goes to bed and sits. He sits in armchair.*) Who's Leontine?

ANGELA. Leontine?

TOM. Yeah, you just went into her; she come after me like the wrath of God.

ANGELA. I never heard that name.

TOM. She's quite a broad.

ANGELA. Why—what'd she say?

TOM. Nothin' much. She sounds like a whore in a house. (*This seems to wilt her a little with yet another grief.*) You really don't remember *none* of it?

ANGELA. (*Pressing her temples apprehensively.*) No. But listen . . . there is always a cruiser, Tom. (*He looks at her, silent.*) I'm telling you, they're down there all the time.

TOM. (*He takes her hand.*) I believe you.

ANGELA. (*Relief and gratitude on her face.*) Even two of them sometimes . . .

17

TOM. Sit down. (*He puts her in a chair, sits opposite her and claps his hands together to inspire hope.*) I have a feeling tonight is going to break the ice.

ANGELA. (*She is glad for their unity, and also digging in against it.*) . . . Just let me get my wind a little.

TOM. Good, get your wind. (*Feeling some semblance of control, he spreads out on the chair, chuckles . . .*) I never knew anybody where everytime I see her there's some big surprise—you're a soap opera. I keep waitin' for the next installment.

ANGELA. (*With tragic pride.*) Yeah, well—I've had a life, kid.

TOM. Like now with these cruisers you keep seein'—

ANGELA. Not that I "keep seeing,"—they're *there.*

TOM. So what you're telling me is—it's the cops that've got you scared. Right? (*She glances at him, loaded with other considerations.*) You wouldn't want to give me a definite yes or no on that. (*She turns to him, her gaze unreadable.*) Okay, then it's yes.

ANGELA. Tom?

TOM. Uh huh?

ANGELA. (*Another message runs parallel with her words.*) You're not realizing the problem . . . (*Slight pause.*) I'm talking about *you.* (*He was momentarily turned away from her; now he faces her. Slight pause.*)

TOM. What about me?

ANGELA. (*Cautiously.*) You've got to start being more careful and watch every step you take . . .

TOM. (*Affects a grin, blushing with anger.*) I hope I'm not hearing this right, Angela.

ANGELA. (*With apology.*) . . . I'm only telling you what I know. You should start being more . . .

TOM. (*Cutting her off.*)—Honey, listen to me. I was a New York cop for twenty-four years; I been threatened by *experts,* so you can imagine that some Mack Sennett Police Department is not my idea of the Holy Terror, y'know? And I wish

you would say this in case somebody should happen to ask
you . . .

ANGELA. (*Trying to be testy.*) . . . Nobody's asking me
anything.

TOM. (*Seething.*) But just in case they did, though — you
tell them that I am on the Epstein case to the end of the bitter
end . . .

ANGELA. . . . I'm not trying to . . .

TOM. . . . And there is nothing anybody can do about that,
Angela — right?

ANGELA. That couldn't be better with me, Tom.

TOM. It wouldn't matter what it was with you, honey, or
with anybody else. Get the picture?

ANGELA. You're one of a kind; honestly, Tom, you really
stand tall. (*She comes to him, kisses him.*) Take me some
place, let me make you happy again. Come on.

TOM. (*Holding both her hands.*) Listen, never be the only
one who knows something . . .

ANGELA. (*Looking contritely at the floor.*) I know . . .

TOM. If somebody else knows it too, that's your best protection. (*She nods agreement. He mimes playing pool.*) The
table's all set up, you want to start hittin' a few? (*The moment of decision is on her, and she gives him a lost smile and
turns away again.*) I know you want to, Angie.

ANGELA. (*A desperate little laugh.*) You know? — Sometimes you talk just like Jimmy Cagney.

TOM. (*Sighs.*) Oh, honey, are we gonna talk about Cagney
now?

ANGELA. Well you do, you get that same sweet-and-sour
thing. And the same brass balls.

TOM. (*Flattered despite himself.*) Well, let's face it, Cagney
was my god. (*Snaps his fingers, still seated he goes into a
light little shuffling tap dance with a chuck of his head.*)
"Take me out to the ball game . . . "

ANGELA. (*Genuinely delighted, relieved.*) Hey,
wonderful!

TOM. Sure, and Pat O'Brien, Spencer Tracey . . . Christ, all those great Irishmen, tough and honest to a man. The movies in them days was Mick-Heaven. The only crooks were Italians.

ANGELA. You'd been great in a movie.

TOM. What as—the dumbest bookie on the block?

ANGELA. No, something dignified—like the first Irish Pope.

TOM. Jesus, you really like me, don't you.

ANGELA. I adore you, Tom. You've saved my life more than you'll ever know. (*She draws him to her on the bed and snuggles onto his lap. He doesn't mind at all, and grins at her.*) Do me once more.

TOM. No more, Ange, I'm sorry—it does something to my judgment.

ANGELA. I could make you fly around the room. You're my ideal, Tom.

TOM. Come on, kid.

ANGELA. You know, Father Paulini once said that if I'd known a man like you earlier in my life, I'd have turned out a completely different person. But once my father'd raped me, I always expected a man to go right for my ass.

TOM. Mmmm.

ANGELA. (*Slaps his cheek lightly.*) Can't you get your mind off the case for *one minute* and just talk to me like a person?

TOM. It's after eleven P.M., Ange, I'm tired.

ANGELA. Know what I love? When you talk about being a copy in the old days in New York. Would you?—It soothes me. Talk about the Communion Breakfasts. (*Rests her head on his chest.*) And how important the Church was, right?

TOM. (*Sighs in boredom—although he likes it, too. He glances down at her, sensing his power . . .*) Oh yeah, the Church was really important in the Department in those days. Like any cop who took money from whores . . . or like dope money . . . the priest lay his head open.

ANGELA. Really? Even dope?

20

TOM. Sure . . . even the Mafia wouldn't touch dope in those days . . .

ANGELA. (*Incredulously.*) Jesus.

TOM. It was a whole different world. (*Grins.*) Like one time they had me guarding the money in the Yankee Stadium office; great big piles of cash on the table. And I ask one of the officials—bein' that they were getting me for nothin', with the city payin' my salary, and all—if I could maybe get a hot dog sent up. So he says sure, gimme fifty cents, I'll send down. Imagine?—I'm watchin' half a million bucks for them and I couldn't even steal a free dog.

ANGELA. I can just see you there . . . with all that money . . . and nobody even giving you a dog. (*Her fear returns in a sweep and she is suddenly welling up.*) Oh, God, Tom . . .

TOM. (*Turning her face to him.*) What is it, honey . . . come on, tell me! (*He hesitates before her vulnerability then suddenly kisses her on the mouth.*)

ANGELA. Come on, Tom—please! Screw me, split me. I'll never forget that last time. You're a bull. Please! I want you! (*He gets to his feet, disturbed by his unforeseen kiss. She is sent into a real outpouring of sobbing—in mourning, as it were, for her wasted life which denied her a man like this . . . he tends to her, smoothing her hair.*)

TOM. Listen now—I could arrange protection. I could have you taken where it's safe. Just tell me what's got you so scared? (*She reaches for him again . . .*) I'd love to, honey, but I'm goddamned if I ever change this subject with you again. It's my professional reputation, my livelihood!

ANGELA. (*Even here there is a faint air of her improvising.*) I'm going to die.

TOM. I hate hearing you say that.

ANGELA. I can't get air. (*Slight pause.*)

TOM. You been to confession?

ANGELA. Yes. But I . . . (*Breaks off.*)

TOM. You couldn't tell him about this, huh? (*Shakes her head.*) I wish I was smarter, kid; I wish I could say the right thing. You don't know how I hate to see you suffering like this.

ANGELA. You've been wonderful, Tom.

TOM. Why can't you give me a little faith? (*A silent struggle in her; she touches his face, then turns away.*) Why are these cops leaning on you, can you just tell me that?

ANGELA. (*She is silent for a moment; some resolve seems to harden.*) Tom.

TOM. I'm listening.

ANGELA. I want you to tell me one thing from the heart. — What's the single main thing you want from this case?

TOM. (*Uncomprehending.*) The single . . . ?

ANGELA. Well is it to get Felix out on the street, or . . . ?

TOM. Well, no, I want the people who put him in there too.

ANGELA. Why? You want revenge or something?

TOM. There's such a thing as the administration of justice, Honey — which in this country, is laying on the floor like a busted dozen eggs, it is a fucking farce. — But I don't think I understand the question.

ANGELA. . . . Nothing. I was just wondering what you wanted.

TOM. Fair enough, — I'll answer you! — Callaghan's got to be blasted out of the prosecutor's office for falsifying evidence, okay? And Bellanca and his whole crew of detectives for conspiring with him . . . (*Grinning.*) Now tell me why you asked a question like that?

ANGELA. Well, I agree with Bellanca . . .

TOM. Why? — Callaghan's worse; publicly calling me a "ridiculous pseudo-detective" and trying to lift my license . . . but we're back in this tic-tac-toe again. Are you going to tell me why the cops are so heavy on you, or not? (*She moves as though framing an answer.*) And I beg you on bended knee, don't start wrappin' me in another ball of wool.

ANGELA. (*Looks down at her hands, almost patently*

22

evading.) The thing, y'see, is that I was so humiliated after what my father . . .

TOM. (*Impatiently.*) Darlin', I *know* your father raped you, but . . .

ANGELA. Oh, am I boring you?

TOM. I didn't say you . . .

ANGELA. (*Fish on the line, she swims away, half-sobbing, half-furious.*) Well, I beg your fucking pardon!

TOM. (*Furiously.*) Angela, I am just about convinced starting this minute that you are full of shit! I don't think you know a goddamned thing about this case and I am going home! Forever! (*He picks up his coat; she grabs him.*)

ANGELA. (*In great alarm.*) Can't we talk for two minutes without the case . . . ?

TOM. I want an answer to what I asked you—what got you into this in the first place? Where are you comin' from, Angela, what is your connection!

ANGELA. (*Gripping her head.*) I'm going crazy!

TOM. I'm turning into a laughing stock! I walk into the Burrington Court House the other day and I had a hard time not to put a fist through some of the stupid smiles on those cops standing around—they all know I'm still on this case after nearly four years . . .

ANGELA. Well, fuck 'em!

TOM. (*Takes a beat—quietly.*) Well, you're really chock full of solutions. I understand a very colorful description of me is goin' around the courthouses—I am the detective who couldn't track a diarrhetic elephant on a glacier.

ANGELA. A diarrhetic elephant . . . ? (*Breaks out laughing.*)

TOM. (*Grinning.*) Gives you a vivid picture, doesn't it? (*Their eyes meet and she sees the steel in his eyes and turns away.*) All right, baby—take care of yourself. I guess tonight ends it between us, kid. And I may as well tell you straight— I am humiliated. (*Waits for her to start it going again; then . . .*) And I'm sorry for your sake; that you couldn't level

23

with me; cause in my opinion, the reason you're sick is that you lie. (*Starts to leave, he sees her near paralysis of fear.*) It's okay. I've got a whole other way to move ahead. It would've been easier with you but I can make it alone. Take care, kid—I'm out of your life. (*He crosses the room to the door, starts getting his arms into his raincoat—stalling, but not too obviously. She watches him in desperation. Her voice trembling, her anxiety pitched high . . .*)

ANGELA. Can you believe . . . ? (*Breaks off.*)

TOM. (*Alerted.*) Believe what, dear?

ANGELA. (*Wringing her hands, struggling in fear of going on . . .*) That a man can be a fine and good man and still do something that's . . . just terrible?

TOM. (*Avid now.*) Sure.

ANGELA. I mean a thing . . . that is not really in his nature to do, but that he has to because . . . it's all so . . . (*Almost crying out.*) . . . rotten in this place?

TOM. (*More warmly now.*) Absolutely. I believe that. If I thought life was straight lines I'd be workin' for the Highway Department. (*Slight pause.*) . . . Like who are you referring to? (*She sends him a terrified glance; there is some longing in her look, too. Her breathing now becomes raspy and he helps her to the bed where she sits, gasping and glancing up at him half in terror and half in hope.*) I always said you had class, darling, you know why?—'Cause of your conscience; most people would just sign out and butter their own potatoes, but not you. You suffer. (*His expectations high, he watches her regain her breathing, but she doesn't venture any further.*) Who were you talking about? (*She glances at him, but nothing more.*) Kid, now listen to me and hold on tight—I am six inches from thinking that *you* were part of the frameup they laid on Felix . . .

ANGELA. (*Furiously.*) How can you be such a stupid son of a bitch!

TOM. . . . And that you're still part of it right now, and trying to keep me from finding out what went down! Which would make you about the lowest cunt since Hitler! (*Pushing up his coat collar.*) Take care of yourself. This time it's for good.

ANGELA. (*With breathless veracity, and really trying not to break down in weeping.*) After five years you don't know the first thing about this case.

TOM. (*Pause. He turns to her at the door.*) . . . Jesus, the way you say that goes right down to my hemorrhoids.

ANGELA. Believe me, darling . . . zee-ro. (*Holds up fore-finger and thumb, touching.*)

TOM. You telling me that Felix Epstein is guilty? (*Long pause.*)

ANGELA. Felix is innocent. (*She heaves for breath; a real attack, she lies down.*)

TOM. (*Goes to her quickly.*) What should I do! You want a doctor? (*She rises on one arm, gasping.*) Tell me what to do! (*She rocks back and forth; he bores in filled with aggressive need.*) All right, can you confirm one fact—did Callaghan fake the picture that nailed Felix? Or don't you know? (*She screams, frightened of him.*)—What are you doing? . . . Oh, no, Angela! (*She presses her fists against her chest and her elbows against her sides with her shoulders pushed upward as though she were trying to become small, like a young child. He recognizes this.*) Don't do that—! Please stop that, Angela! (*He makes a move toward her.*)

ANGELA. Don't you touch me! (*She skitters into a corner, blindly staring at him.*)

TOM. (*Reaching toward her protectively.*) Ange . . . (*With a frightened scream, she cowers all scrunched up, terror in her face. A sound from her mouth, high and childlike.*) Is it "Emily"?

ANGELA. Don't, please . . . . !

TOM. Okay, Emily . . . (*Opening his coat and holding out his palms.*) . . . see? Nothin' on me at all. Okay, darling? Why don't you come out and we get a little ice cream from the corner? Your father's gone, honey—honest, he won't be comin' back tonight. (*He takes one step toward her but she reacts in fright so he backs up.*) Okay, dear, you stay there and I'll just make a call, okay? Take your time, have a little nap if you want. (*Goes and sits beside phone, dials. As he waits, he playfully twiddles his fingers at her.*) Hya, darlin'. (*Into phone.*) Sorry to bother you again, Mrs. Levy . . . thanks a lot. (*To Angela.*) How about a chocolate fudge later? — I'm sorry, Josh, — No, no, I hate to bother you so late . . . — Oh, zonked out again, being Emily now, all scrunched up like an eight year old, it's pathetic. Listen, bad news . . . she claims it's the cops leaning on her. — I think it could be, yes. But she's been seeing two police cruisers parked on the block every night . . . but I looked and there's none down there, you see? But why do I still believe her? — Oh absolutely! I believe her, Josh! — Except if it was just that I invested so much in her I could walk away; wasting your time is most of what you do in this business. (*Listens, a rapt stare now.*) Now *that's* funny; I was thinking of Maria all the way down in the car before, like she was sitting in the seat beside me. — There is a similarity, yes; the same kind of sexiness, maybe. (*Glances up at Angela. A shake of the head, wondrously.*) — So in other words, I've blown four and a half years . . . on a dream! (*Resistance hardens his face.*) Except, goddamit, Josh, she was the first one who told me about Carl Linstrom; — yes, the man who was seen covered with blood, running away from the Kaplan house. And now I have four separate witnesses to corroborate and I can't get the police to make an arrest! You see what I mean? — She knows too many facts for just a crazy, fantasizing whore. . . ! (*Angela sits up, he sees her.*) . . . We're back on the air, I'll be in touch. (*Hangs up. She approaches him, staring.*) Well! What do you say, Bubbles — welcome back! (*She stares at him, puzzled, suspicious. He is defensive . . .*) I made a little call. (*Her stare is unrelenting.*) To my friend, the psychiatrist. Sends his regards. (*Her stare remains.*) I told you — he's my quarterback sometimes. He's still very interested in the case . . . You know, Felix being Jewish . . .

ANGELA. Some Jew! He didn't have the balls to join my

committee.

TOM. Well, let's face it, kid, neither did anybody else, that was a one-woman committee. (*Stands.*) Well, take care. I really got to hit the pike.

ANGELA. Wait, wait . . . we didn't even talk. What've you been working on lately?

TOM. Oh, nothing great.

ANGELA. Like what?

TOM. Corporation stuff mostly. Big ball bearing company; in fact—I've got to go out to Phoenix, investigate a guy they're about to make the vice president.

ANGELA. They still doing that shit?

TOM. (*Shrugs.*) Well, you know—you can't have a homosexual vice president of a ball bearing company.

ANGELA. But how do you do that?

TOM. Ah, it's boring. I get his old airplane ticket stubs for the past few months; they usually travel on the company account; and see if he's been to some off-the-track town . . . you know, Ashtabula, Ohio; Grim City, Iowa; and I go to the gay bar and show the bartender his picture with a hundred dollar bill clipped to it, and he tells me if he's ever seen him there. I didn't used to mind it, but I don't like it anymore. But . . . (*Shrugs, with a sigh, rubbing two fingers together.*)

ANGELA. And for that he can't be vice president?

TOM. Well, they're scared of blackmail. And you know, he's supposed to be a good example.

ANGELA. To who?

TOM. Who the hell knows anymore? (*At the door.*)

ANGELA. (*The same lostness and tension grip her but she no longer pleads for him to stay.*) Would you take another look down the street before you go?

TOM. For you, I'll do it. (*He goes, opens door, exits. She remains absolutely still, facing front. He returns.*) I don't see them.

ANGELA. (*Awakened.*) Heh?

TOM. There's no cruiser down there.

27

ANGELA. Who?

TOM. (*Impatiently.*) The cruiser! The cops you were so worried about.

ANGELA. (*Preoccupied.*) Oh.

TOM. "Oh!"—Five minutes ago you were . . . Oh, forget it. I don't see Philly in the living room. So why don't you try to relax now, okay?—Maybe I'll see you sometime. (*She is lost in thought. He turns her face to him.*) . . . Ange?

ANGELA. I used to be with Charley.

TOM. (*Electrified.*) . . . Callaghan? (*She is silent.*) Talking about the Prosecutor?

ANGELA. (*Hard as a nail.*) I will deny everything if you ever try to hurt him with it.—I'm myself now, Tom, you understand what I'm saying to you? I will never hurt Charley. (*Takes a sudden inhale.*)

TOM. (*Stunned.*) Okay.—Was this like one or two shots or . . . ?

ANGELA. Three, four times a week over two years. We went to Canada and Puerto Rico, couple of times.

TOM. And when did it end? (*Slight pause.*)

ANGELA. He's come back to me.

TOM. You seeing him *now*?

ANGELA. (*A sudden expressiveness, closeness.*) He's the love of my life, Tom.

TOM. Right.—This is quite a blow to my mind, darlin'. (*Slight pause.*) You mean like . . . you were exercising with him while he was prosecuting Felix?

ANGELA. Yes. (*Slight pause.*)—You don't believe me.

TOM. (*Slight pause.*) Well . . . it sure ties certain things together. That's the reason you came to the trial every day, is that it?—to buck him up?

ANGELA. (*Hesitation.*) I wasn't there to buck him up. (*Slight pause.*) I was there taking notes—which you saw me do, and which you read.

TOM. (*Apologetically.*) That's right, honey . . .

ANGELA. Some whores can take notes, y'know—I went to Mary Immaculate, which just happens to have the highest

28

academic record in the state. I can also add, subtract and multiply . . .

TOM. Now, don't go off into a . . .

ANGELA. (*Deeply agitated.*) Sometimes I don't understand why the fuck I talk to you at all, O'Toole. I mean, Jesus . . . (*He lets her find her calm as she walks about shaking her head.*) I may come off the street but that don't mean I've still got rocks in my head. I'm going to get out of this situation, you know.

TOM. I hope so, Angela. — Out of what situation?

ANGELA. (*Retreating.*) Never mind. Just don't forget what I said about hurting Charley. I can murder you if you do that.

TOM. How you going to murder me, Ange?

ANGELA. Don't worry, I can do it.

TOM. We're gonna forget you said that, okay?

ANGELA. I'm not threatening you!

TOM. The second time tonight . . .

ANGELA. I didn't mean that I . . .

TOM. Stop-right-here-Angela! Charley Callaghan has tried to get my Investigator's License lifted because I have gotten reversals on two of his biggest cases, just like I am going to do on this one . . .

ANGELA. I did not mean . . . !

TOM. . . . So you can ask me not to hurt Charley but please do not try to scare me with him because that is to laugh! Now what'd you want to say? — I mean I hope you are not conveying some kind of a threat from somebody.

ANGELA. You know? — Sometimes I think you ought to see a psychiatrist.

TOM. Oy gevalt! — Kid, you are going to end me up pluckin' chickens in the funny farm!

ANGELA. But you suspect everything I say! You tell me to trust you, but do you trust me?

TOM. Darlin', look — let's get back to you taking those notes during the trial; can I ask what they were for?

ANGELA. 'Cause I knew Felix had nothing to do with Kaplan's murder, and I wanted to prove it.

TOM. I'm still not getting the picture, dear, forgive me. You were in the hammock with Charley at nights and in the days taking notes to *dis*prove his case?

ANGELA. We broke up over the case.

TOM. (*Impressed.*) Oh!

ANGELA. I couldn't stand what it was doing to him. He'd come back from the court and we'd go out to the beach and build a fire and he'd stare into it with tears pouring down his cheeks. Sometimes he would look up to the stars and try to pray. Charley studied for the priesthood, you know . . .

TOM. I heard that.

ANGELA. He still does retreats.

TOM. Yeah, well . . . I guess I must've missed his spiritual side.

ANGELA. You have a closed mind: I'm telling you he's a whole other person than you believe.

TOM. Listen, I'm always ready to learn. — What were the tears for, though?

ANGELA. . . . We even went to churches in San Juan.

TOM. Together?

ANGELA. Well, we sat in different parts . . .

TOM. In other words, the tears were that he was rigging the Epstein case, or what?

ANGELA. (*She doesn't answer at once.*)

TOM. Ange? Please. — What were the tears?

ANGELA. It wasn't his fault. The Chief of Detectives handed him the case, all tied with a ribbon and ready for trial . . .

TOM. Bellanca. (*Angela nods.*) So *Bellanca* faked the photograph? (*She nods again.*)

ANGELA. Charley didn't want to touch the case. They made him push it. I know how you hate him, Tom, but you have to believe me . . .

TOM. Tell me something — why did they pick on Felix in the first place? Why him?

ANGELA. Total accident — he just happened to have come to town to visit his uncle, Abe Kaplan; it's exactly like he claimed—he was trying to get Kaplan to take him into the accountancy firm.

TOM. But why did they have to go through that whole charade when they could just have gone out and picked up Linstrom?—They had to know Linstrom was covered with blood that night—they *had* the killer any time they wanted him.

ANGELA. (*Slight pause.*) Because Linstrom was a runner.

TOM. A runner?

ANGELA. For Kaplan. (*Slight pause.*)

TOM. Abe Kaplan was in drugs?

ANGELA. In!—Abe *ran* the drugs in this town.—God, you are stupid. You're pathetic.

TOM. (*Embarrassed.*) I knew Abe was the big loan shark . . .

ANGELA. That was the front.

TOM. . . . So they latched onto Felix . . . tell me again, will ya?

ANGELA. (*Impatiently.*) To make it look like a family argument—the uncle and the nephew . . .

TOM. But Charley's the chief . . . (*She silently assents.*) . . . if he felt so bad about it, why did he have to go ahead and make the case against Felix?

ANGELA. (*She is staring.*)

TOM. Don't go out on me, will you? (*She stares. He bursts out.*) This is horrendous.—You cannot go out on me now! Why couldn't they arrest Lindstrom?

ANGELA. Because it could open the whole can of worms.

TOM. What can is that, Honey?

ANGELA. (*This is deeper than she wanted to go. Barely audible.*) The police connection.

TOM. To the drugs.

ANGELA. That's why they're parking down there. (*He gives her an evasive nod.*) They are, you know. (*He gives her a deeper nod of assuagement. But his thought has moved to something else at which he stares now . . .*) They are parking down there, Tom . . . (*She starts angrily for the door, but he forces her into an embrace.*)

TOM. If I was to ask you, Angela—how do you know Abe Kaplan was in drugs . . . can I ask you that?

ANGELA. (*She doesn't answer at once, moving away from him.*)

TOM. . . . Because I'm trying to be as objective as I can, you see, dear? I mean let's face it, Abe was one of the pillars, right? With the synagogue and the Boys Town and you name it, and a lot of people are going to find that hard to believe, you know?

ANGELA. (*Decides, faces him.*) I used to be with Abe.

TOM. (*Rocked.*) . . . No kiddin'. *Abe?*

ANGELA. A lot. We went down to Bimini together.

TOM. Bimini.

ANGELA. Twenty, twenty-five times.

TOM. Isn't Bimini one of the . . . ?

ANGELA. I carried for him coming back. I would deliver the stuff to Bellanca. (*A long pause. He moves now, facing front.*) That's why I'm so upset with them parking down there, you see?

TOM. (*He sets his jaw.*) But they are not parking down there, Honey.

ANGELA. (*Springing up, gripping her head.*) They are parking down there!! (*He shuts his eyes.*) And you . . . you've got to start taking precautions.

TOM. We must be on some kind of wave length together . . . (*He takes a snubnose revolver out of his pocket.*) I never carry this, but I'm leaving the house tonight and, for some reason . . . I stuck it in my pocket going out the door. (*Puts gun away.*) Incidentally, if Bellanca's holding any kind of . . . like a drug rap over you, the best thing you could do is level with me, you know; the Feds would protect a witness against drug dealers, they have a witness-protection program and it's serious . . . You're not going out on me, are you?

ANGELA. —No, I'm here. (*Her voice breaks in the tension and she moves, holding down a sobbing fit.*)

TOM. How long can you go on with this tension? You're going to explode. (*She simply shakes her head.*) Has anybody said exactly what they want from you? — Is it to get me to stop coming around? — or what?

ANGELA. (*Staring ahead, almost stupidly.*) For me to give him his letters back.

TOM. (*This is new . . . he uses a fine degree of charm.*) . . . Which letters we talkin' about? (*She stares.*) Charley wrote you letters? (*She turns to him blankly.*) About your relationship, or what?

ANGELA. About his struggle.

TOM. Like with his conscience. (*She is staring ahead.*) He wrote you a letter about it?

ANGELA. (*Nodding.*) Nine.

TOM. No kiddin' — (*With the faintest tinge of doubt now.*) — nine letters?

ANGELA. (*Reaches for his hand.*) Don't leave me, Tom.

TOM. I'm with you, Ange. And where are they — these letters?

ANGELA. . . . I have them some place.

TOM. Oh.

ANGELA. I always had to have candles for him in the apartment.

TOM. Candles.

ANGELA. It helped him — to look into flames. I was the closest to him, closer than his wife. He couldn't keep it to himself anymore. I begged him. I prayed for him but he had to push the case, or he'd lose everything. I told him, I said, "You could be anything, you could be President of the United States! — Don't do this to an innocent man, God will take it out of your flesh!" — I thought if he saw me in court taking notes he'd realize that I meant business and I would not let Felix rot in jail . . . and it would make him stop the case. (*She breathes in suddenly, deeply, and the eyes seem to be going blind.*)

TOM. Don't leave me, Angela.

ANGELA. (*Gripping his hand.*) I'm staying. I'm trying . . . Oh, God, Tom, you don't know, you don't know . . .

TOM. Tell me, what, what?

ANGELA. . . . They picked me up off the street today. (*She is in open terror.*)

TOM. Cops?

ANGELA. I lied to you before . . . When I was walking past Ramsey's piano store, they suddenly came up beside me and jammed me into the cruiser, and drove me around, two cops and a detective. Caught my hair in the goddamned door!

TOM. Bastards! — What'd they want?

ANGELA. That if I didn't straighten up I'd be floating in the bay. (*She weeps. He holds her in his arms.*)

TOM. (*He turns toward the door.*) So they're leaning on you for the letters, is that bottom line? (*Angela nods.*) Why don't you give them to them?

ANGELA. But I'd never see him again.

TOM. You honest to God see him now?

ANGELA. He comes, once or twice a week. But now it's only to get them back.

TOM. You're not making it with him anymore.

ANGELA. Only once in a while. (*Now she curls up on the bed.*)

TOM. Can I see the letters? (*She doesn't react.*) You want to go somewhere? My valise is in the car. (*She stretches a hand to him, tempted, conflicted.*) Get your coat on, come on, we'll ride somewhere and talk more. (*He holds her hand.*)

ANGELA. I'll die before I hurt him, Tom.

TOM. All right — Suppose you don't show me anything, just read me the relevant parts — you keep them in your hands. — Go on, get them. (*She is in a fever of indecision. Gets off the bed, one moment covering her eyes with her hands, the next, glancing at him as though trying to judge him. She opens drawer off dressing table; hesitates, then takes out a brush and brushes her hair.*) Darlin', listen to me — with that kind of evidence, I can put Felix back on the street by noon tomorrow.

ANGELA. (*Pressed.*) I said I can't hurt Charley!

TOM. (*Furiously.*) Then why've you told me this?

ANGELA. I can't give you them now.

TOM. When then?

ANGELA. When I can! (*He watches her for a long moment.*)

TOM. Angela — explain to me — why'd you tell me all this?

ANGELA. So you'd help me!

TOM. Help you how? (*She looks directly into his eyes in an open appeal.*) Are you telling me to drop Felix? You're not telling me that, are you? (*She is silent.*) Honey — you mean I just drive home now and go to sleep? (*She is silent — furiously.*) Talk to me.

ANGELA. (*Scared of him now.*) I don't owe Felix Epstein — I fought for him!

TOM. How! You had a cannon and you threw some bean-bags! And for five whole years you cold-bloodedly watched me chasing up one deadend after another and never said boo about this?

ANGELA. You never trusted a word I said, did you? Do you trust me even now? You know you don't!

TOM. What other man in your life ever believed in you like I did! How dare you say that to me! I'm damn near a laughing stock for believing in you. — Now give it to me straight — did you call me here tonight to get me to quit this case? (*The load on her is crushing . . .*)

ANGELA. Sssssh! — Don't talk so loud . . .

TOM. (*To the door.*) Fuck Philly and fuck them! (*The violence in the air sends her into quicker movements seeking escape and air . . .*) Where are you comin' from, Angela, whose side are you on? What is happening here? (*With a cry in his voice, he grips her.*) Are they running you? Do they make you keep calling me?

ANGELA. (*Violently breaking from him, shaking a finger at him.*) You know . . . you know . . . (*Groping breathlessly, she becomes rigidly straight; a new personality, a terribly austere, dignified lady with upper class speech.*) . . . it might just be a terribly good idea for you to think a little more highly of me and stop irritating me!

TOM. Who's this now?

ANGELA. You are irritating me!

TOM. I refuse to talk to Renata!

ANGELA. Stop irritating me!

TOM. (*Even though knowing she is hardly able to hear him — in fact, she is softly hooting to herself as he speaks in order to block off his sounds and mock him.*) Irritating *you!* You knew all these years where the bodies were buried and I'm irritating you? You're lucky I quit the booze, your face'd be running down that wall by now! (*Swelling, pulling up his pants.*) The enormity!

ANGELA. Enormity? (*She bursts out laughing rather merrily.*)

TOM. And what if I don't quit? Would that . . . put you in some kind of an emergency?

ANGELA. (*As though quite beyond all harm.*) Me!

TOM. . . . In other words, sweetie . . . are you trying to tell me that we're not really all that great friends? — Is that it?

ANGELA. (*Confused, but adopting an indignant stance.*) Now you listen . . . !

TOM. You listen to me — this is still the United States of America, you don't have to lay down in front of those punks.

ANGELA. Well, I must say . . . what astounds *me* is how you get to think *you're* such a high grade cultured individual and such a great Catholic . . . !

TOM. All right, Renata, come! I'll find a doctor for you in Boston.

ANGELA. . . . But all you really are is guttural!

TOM. Will you just blow that out your ass and talk straight?

ANGELA. . . . You can't help it, your whole manner is guteral because your whole background is guttural.

TOM. You're not even using the word right.

ANGELA. I mean who do you imagine you fuckin' are — just because you read some magazines without any pictures?

TOM. (*Eyes rolling upward.*) Jesus Christ . . .

ANGELA. *You* have the audacious contempt to call the Lord's name in vain?

TOM. (*Defeated.*) Okay, Renata, let's just forget the

36

whole . . .

ANGELA. *You* can call me Miss Marshall. Stupid bastard.

TOM. (*Laughs, despite everything.*) By this time Miss
Renata Marshall ought to know that a respectable lady like
her doesn't call people stupid bastards.

ANGELA. Which I would be delighted to do if these stupid
bastards had the mental competence to understand any other
kind of language, you dumb shit.

TOM. Touche. (*Spreads his arms out.*) Okay, pull out the
nails, I want to come down. I'm through, hon . . . for
tonight. But I'll be back and we can start *all over again*! (*She
is surprised, frightened too as the air goes out of her. In a
mixture of laughter and fury . . .*) That's right, Baby. (*Partly
toward the door.*) I will never give up until Felix Epstein is
walking the street! Plus lover-boy Callaghan gets a long number across the back of his shirt — if, in fact, you ever really laid
him at all outside of your mental waterbed!

ANGELA. (*Exhausted, she starts to droop.*) Well, you don't
say . . .

TOM. Then where's his letters? Show me one single proof
that this is not another one of your spitball delusions?

ANGELA. *My* delusions! *My* delusions! And what about
your delusions? All of a sudden *I'm in the United States of
America*? (*Tears are pouring into her eyes.*) And *I've* got
delusions? This town is in the United States? This police
force . . . ?

TOM. (*His pain surges and he protectively embraces her,
chastened.*) I gotcha, Honey.

ANGELA. (*Weeping.*) Help me — for Christ's sake, Tom!

TOM. Sssh! (*He cuts off her weeping by kissing her mouth
and holds her against himself with great force. And turning
her face up . . .*) Did you really think you could get me off
the case?

ANGELA. (*Covers her face and sobs in defeat.*) My God!
(*The phone rings: They are both caught off guard. She goes
and picks up the phone with high tension, her voice fearful,
very faint — clearly, she has some specific caller in mind.*)

37

Yes? (*Surprised and pleased — charm suddenly warms her voice.*) Oh! — Oh, I'm so sorry, I forgot all about it! (*A near stutter.*) Well . . . well . . . well, yes, sure . . . (*Looks confused at her watch but can't quite focus on it . . . and with a glance at Tom,* sotto voce.) What's the time?

TOM. (*Sotto voce.*) Ten to twelve.

ANGELA. (*With a warmly thankful glance at him.*) Sure, I can make it, I just have to get dre . . . (*But glancing down at herself, she breaks off.*) . . . in fact, I am dressed already . . . (*Feels her hair, surprised that it is in place.*) . . . in fact, my hair's practically done . . . Ah . . . (*Ineffectually shielding the phone — oddly — with a half-turn away from Tom.*) . . . where is it again? Oh, right! (*Nearly whispering.*) And what's the room? Okay. (*Smiles.*) . . . You too, pussycat! (*Hangs up. She has expanded with a new pleasure-shame, an identify that is palpable. She turns to face him.*) I had an appointment I forgot all about.

TOM. You did? How come?

ANGELA. I don't know, I just blew it.

TOM. They say that means a person really doesn't want to go.

ANGELA. You got time to drop me?

TOM. (*This is more difficult.*) . . . Where's that?

ANGELA. (*Evasively.*) Well . . . like corner of Main and Benson would be okay.

TOM. (*An instant — he looks at her almost incredulous, then turns away, and with dry rage, humilitation.*) Come on.

ANGELA. (*With fresh energy.*) Just got to fix my face, be right with you. Put your feet up. (*She turns to go up to the bathroom.*)

TOM. (*With an open resentment.*) Why don't I drop you right at the hotel instead of on the street — it's only a few more yards? (*She turns back to him, ashamed — as it were — for his sake.*)

ANGELA. . . . The corner would be okay. (*He doesn't reply, his head turned angrily away from her, although he is attempting to grin. She breaks the moment, hurries into the bathroom . . . another moment . . . and in a dispirited way he picks up the phone and dials. He waits, greatly tired, an inward look in his deadened face.)*

TOM. This could be tapped, you want to hang up? — Good, turn it on. You rolling? *(As for a record.)* Abe Kaplan was hit by one of his own crazy runners. — That's correct, he was into drugs, Josh . . . with the detective squad. — Why is it incredible? — Because she was Abe's broad. And Callaghan's too, incidentally. *(Listens.)* Look, talk to you later, I just wanted to tell you this much before I go outside. — No don't worry. I'll be all right — What do you want me to do, call the police? — Well, that's nice of you to offer, but she's only going to twist you around too, isn't she? I mean I've got to stop looking for some red tag that says "Real" on it; I don't have the education, but I have the feeling and I'm just going to have to follow my nose, wherever it takes me, y'know? — If it's real for me then that's the last question I can ask, right? — Well, I'm not sure yet, but somehow I think I can decide pretty quick now, maybe tonight. — I do, yes . . . I feel kind of relieved now that I've thought of this. And at the same time like in a fog on top of a mountain where the next step is either six inches down or five thousand feet. *(A laugh.)* — It *is* a mystery, but I still have my ignoramous opinion, Josh; I think that somewhere way upstream the corruption is poisoning the water and making us all a little crazy. — Her? No, she's feeling great now! In the toilet getting saddled up for some honcho in the Hilton, and ten minutes ago gasping out her last and final breath! *(Laughs.)* — No, kid, it's not unreal, it's just horrendous! *(Angela enters.)* . . . And here she comes now, riding on her elephant, our Lady of the Hilton, looking like seven million bucks! *(She laughs delightedly.)* You hear her? She's laughing, fulla beans.

ANGELA. *(Calls into phone.)* Hya, Doc!

TOM. Now if only Felix could get the joke? — Right, talk to you soon. *(Hangs up.)*

ANGELA. Before we go down — if those cops give me any trouble, we're going to midnight mass at St. Jude's, okay?

(*He laughs brazenly.*) What are you laughing at?

TOM. What cops?

ANGELA. (*Gesturing toward door.*) In the cruiser downstairs.

TOM. (*Totally loose and lost, he laughs.*) What cruiser downstairs? (*She looks shaken, distraught.*) You stole five years of my life, you goddamn lunatic! I ought to wrap you around a lamp post.

ANGELA. (*Gathering herself in protest.*) But there's always one there!

TOM. (*Mimicking.*) "There's always one there!" (*Clenching his fists to keep them off her.*) How did you get into my life!! (*With a look of apprehensive uncertainty mixed with indignation, she turns and dashes out the door. He strides about, full of self-hatred.*) How did I get into this goddamn dream! My brain died! She murdered my brain . . . ! (*She enters, rather slowly, glancing at him with a new air of mock indignation. He reads this look, and takes an uncertain few steps toward the door, then halts and turns back to see her looking at herself in her hand mirror with bland assurance. He rushes out the door. She stares front. He re-enters.*)

ANGELA. Who's crazy now?

TOM. Angela . . . Christ, I'm sorry. Forgive me, will you? (*She gives him a peeved look. Approaching her, arms extended . . .*) Oh, Darlin' . . . Oh, Ange . . . I can't help it, I love you! (*He starts to embrace her but she frees herself.*)

ANGELA. Hey, watch the hair, for Christ sake! I'm serious, you've got to get yourself some help!

TOM. (*Apologetically.*) But, honey, they weren't down there a little while ago . . .

ANGELA. Well, don't cops take leaks?

TOM. (*Anxious to forestall.*) Look . . . what do you say we go and get a ravioli and a nice bottle of wine . . . ?

ANGELA. (*Imperatively.*) I have to go!

TOM. (*Surprising himself, a cry.*) *Why*! They don't have to run *every thing* in this world! . . . Listen . . . get in my car. Let me take you to Judge McGuire's house—you remember,

40

he and I are close; he'll arrange federal protection; we can bust this case and you can . . . you can start a whole new life, darling. (*She stares into his face.*) And who knows, maybe we could still walk off into that sunset together? (*Taking her hand.*)

ANGELA. I can't.

TOM. Yes you could, if you believed in me.

ANGELA. No, not only you, Tommy, — I think you got me too late; all that went by. Come on, I'm late. (*Takes coat off a chair, she starts U. He rushes to intercept her.*)

TOM. Wait! I want to tell you something Dr. Levy told me.

ANGELA. Levy! Levy's gutless.

TOM. He said I haven't been in love since I was twenty-five, so you like woke me from the dead, sexually, so . . .

ANGELA. Did he really say that?

TOM. So I handed you almost magical powers, like you could see in the dark through a slab of concrete.

ANGELA. Oh, Tommy . . .

TOM. . . . But I see now that whatever you know you're never going to tell me, because you don't want me off and away. That's it, isn't it — never, never, never.

ANGELA. Listen! — maybe if we could meet for a good long lunch tomorrow . . .

TOM. No more lunches!

ANGELA. Give me one more chance to try to tell you, Tommy; that makes me happier than anything I've ever heard in my life — that I woke you from the dead. How about Pinnochio's, one o'clock?

TOM. No! Come, I'll drop you. I've got a man in jail. I've wasted too much time. (*He gets his coat and hat.*)

ANGELA. So this is it, then?

TOM. This has to be the last long night, yes. But you get evidence, something I can take into court, call me anytime — I just have to get to work, okay?

ANGELA. Okay. Then I should tell you something to keep in mind. There's a whole side of this case you never even heard of. (*He goes stock still.*) Don't believe it, I don't

41

care — but I have to tell you. You're not just leaving a crazy woman, you're leaving the case. 'Cause I'm the only only one alive who knows. There are names that'd knock your head off, all the way to Boston, Washington, Providence and New York. The whole criminal justice system could be picked up by the tail like a dead rat. All you got now is the tip of the tip of the iceberg. — Good Luck. (*She opens the door and glances back.*) You still dropping me or is that out too? (*She sees him wipe a tear from his eye.*) What're you doing? (*Comes to him, incredulously.*) Why are you crying?

TOM. (*Shrugs, shakes his head.*) . . . I guess because I still believe you.

ANGELA. (*She draws his face to her and holds him.*) I'll be at the corner table at the end of the bar.

TOM. NO!

ANGELA. Please come! (*Lowers her hands.*) Please come! It's all in me Tom. And you're the only one who can ever get it out. I want to talk . . . quietly and . . . honestly. (*She is staring ahead.*) And then maybe it'll all be there . . . all the rottenness is going to drop away. And then, maybe I could start to change my life. I'm going to expect you. You might just be amazed! (*She goes out. From the next room . . .*) Philly? Where are you? I'll be back in a couple of hours! (*Calling.*) Tom? Are you coming?

TOM. (*Eyes lifted.*) Sorry, Felix . . . but hold on, don't let go, baby!

ANGELA. (*From further off, calling.*) What are you doing, you're making me late!

TOM. (*Shutting his eyes.*) Dear God . . . make it only one more time!

ANGELA. Tom!

TOM. Yes! Coming, coming, coming . . . (*Hurrying out as the scene quickly blacks out.*)

END

PROP AND FURNITURE PRE-SET

Swivel Armchair R.
  On offstage arm:
    Ashtray with water (no butts)
    Cigarettes
    Lighter
  On back of chair:
    Printed skirt
    Garter belt
    Fur pillow
    Rust pillow
    Angela's black coat
  Under chair:
    Pink printed shirt
Floor lamp U.
Wastebasket R. of floor lamp with dressing
Vanity U.C.
  On R. side:
    Glass with lime
    Ashtray with water
    Dressing
  On C. part:
    Club soda
    Dressing
    Strike extra kleenexes

On L. side:
   Angela's purse with compact
In L. drawer:
   Brush
Dresser U.C.
   On:
      Picture
      Angela's gloves
      Vase with feathers
      Black panties
      Perfume atomizer
      White scarf
      Ashtray with water
      Fan
   In 2nd drawer:
      Angela's black striped dress
      Dressing
Bed C.
   On:
      5 Curlers (1 hidden under covers)
      National Inquirer U.L.
      People Magazine D.R.
      Cosmopolitan Magazine D.R.
      White skirt D.R.
      Covers pulled down
      10 pillows piled into headboard
      Shawl draped over headboard
   On floor D.R. of Bed:
      1 Black skirt
      1 Cream blouse
      Tan pants
      Purple shirt
   R. of Bed:
      Slippers
   L. under bed:
      Black shoes (Angela's)

Bed table R. Bed
   On:
      Ashtray with wet paper towel and 4 butts
Stool L.
   On:
      Red sweater
Throw rug L.
      On D. edge:
      Pantyhose
Chair L.
   On back:
      Blue sweater
      Rust bra
      Leopard pillow
      Fur throw
Table D.L.
   On:
      Phone with cord loose
      Check cord
   Under:
      Kleenex box
      Dressing
Offstage table L.:
      Tan bag
      Hankerchief
      Cigarette
      Lighter
      Spritzer bottle
      Flashlight
Blinds on L. Window down 3/4 with 1 blind twisted
R. door closed *not locked*
L. door closed
In dressing room to be set later for Angela's quick change:
      Make up
      Wig brush
      Flower comb

        Earrings
        Extra barretts
        Bra
        Wet kleenex
Personals:
    Tom:
        Black notebook in left coat pocket
        Glasses in right pocket
        Gun
        Watch
        Wedding ring
    Angela:
        Watch
        Roller with clip
        Cross necklace

COSTUME LIST

Tom

Tan overcoat
Blue cardigan
Green sport shirt
Dark green slacks
Black socks
Grey "Hugh Puppies" shoes
Grey tweed rain hat

Angela

Wig
Pink robe
Black bra
Black slip
Black pantyhose
Black panties
Gold watch
Gold cross necklace
Rhinestone barrets
Flowered hair piece
Rhinestone earrings
Black and white striped dress
Black shoes

TODAY'S HOTTEST NEW PLAYS

❑ **THREE VIEWINGS by Jeffrey Hatcher.** Three comic-dramatic monologues, set in a midwestern funeral parlor, interweave as they explore the ways we grieve, remember, and move on. *"Finally, what we have been waiting for: a new, true, idiosyncratic voice in the theater. And don't tell me you hate monologues; you can't hate them more than I do. But these are much more: windows into the deep of each speaker's fascinating, paradoxical, unique soul, and windows out into a gallery of surrounding people, into hilarious and horrific coincidences and conjunctions, into the whole dirty but irresistible business of living in this damnable but spellbinding place we presume to call the world."* - New York Magazine. [1M, 2W]

❑ **HAVING OUR SAY by Emily Mann.** The Delany Sisters' Bestselling Memoir is now one of Broadway's Best-Loved Plays! Having lived over one hundred years apiece, Bessie and Sadie Delany have plenty to say, and their story is not simply African-American history or women's history...it is our history as a nation. *"The most provocative and entertaining family play to reach Broadway in a long time."* - New York Times. *"Fascinating, marvelous, moving and forceful."* - Associated Press. [2W]

❑ **THE YOUNG MAN FROM ATLANTA Winner of the 1995 Pulitzer Prize. by Horton Foote.** An older couple attempts to recover from the suicide death of their only son, but the menacing truth of why he died, and what a certain Young Man from Atlanta had to do with it, keeps them from the peace they so desperately need. *"Foote ladles on character and period nuances with a density unparalleled in any living playwright."* - NY Newsday. [5M, 4W]

❑ **SIMPATICO by Sam Shepard.** Years ago, two men organized a horse racing scam. Now, years later, the plot backfires against the ringleader when his partner decides to come out of hiding. *"Mr. Shepard writing at his distinctive, savage best."* - New York Times. [3M, 3W]

❑ **MOONLIGHT by Harold Pinter.** The love-hate relationship between a dying man and his family is the subject of Harold Pinter's first full-length play since *Betrayal*. *"Pinter works the language as a master pianist works the keyboard."* - New York Post. [4M, 2W, 1G]

❑ **SYLVIA by A.R. Gurney.** This romantic comedy, the funniest to come along in years, tells the story of a twenty-two year old marriage on the rocks, and of Sylvia, the dog who turns it all around. *"A delicious and dizzy new comedy."* - New York Times. *"FETCHING! I hope it runs longer than Cats!"* - New York Daily News. [2M, 2W]

DRAMATISTS PLAY SERVICE, INC.
440 Park Avenue South, New York, New York 10016 212-683-8960 Fax 212-213-1539